*So remember while December*
*Brings the Christmas day,*
*In the year let there be Christmas*
*In the things you do and say;*
*Wouldn't life be worth the living*
*Wouldn't dreams be coming true*
*If we kept the Christmas spirit*
*All the whole year through!*

*— Anonymous*

# Keep
# Christmas
## in Your Heart

A Collection of Writings
in Celebration of the Holiday Season

Edited by Gary Morris

**Blue Mountain Press**™
Boulder, Colorado

Library of Congress Control Number: 2003091344
ISBN: 0-88396-749-9

ACKNOWLEDGMENTS appear on page 48.

Certain trademarks are used under license.

Manufactured in Thailand.
First Printing: 2003

This book is printed on recycled paper.

**Blue Mountain Arts**®
P.O. Box 4549, Boulder, Colorado 80306

# Contents

(Authors listed in order of first appearance)

# How to Keep Christmas in Your Heart...

1. **Shine**... with your God-given talents.

2. **Sparkle**... with interest when you listen to others.

3. **Twinkle**... with a sense of humor, and you'll never take life too seriously.

4. **Sing**... to keep up your spirits.

5. **Pray**... and you'll know you're never alone.

6. **Unwrap**... your dreams and make them happen.

7. **Celebrate**... your every step to success.

8. **Decorate**... your own space and make it your peaceful retreat.

9. **Play**... with passion after you work hard.

10. **Exchange**... your doubts for hopes, your frowns for smiles.

11. **Make**... cookies, friends, happiness.

12. **Believe**... in the spirit of Santa Claus and in your power to make the world a better place.

— Jacqueline Schiff

# If I Could, I Would Give You All These Things for Christmas

*I* wanted to wrap up the greatest of smiles, one that stretched from ear to ear, so that you would know how happy it makes me to know that you are in the world. I was hoping then that your Christmas would be filled with smiles and happiness, too.

I wanted to send you the warmest of hugs, one that could squeeze you especially tight. Then you would feel comfort both inside and out and know you are extra loved.

I wanted to give you my heart to hold on to
for the times when you don't feel like feeling,
so you could be happy today and always, and
never feel sad again. Then my heart would
feel complete being so close to your own.

I wanted to catch a twinkling star, one that
would shine especially for you, and place it
in your hands. It would be a guiding light
and make your day much brighter. Then you
could make a million wishes that would all
come true.

I want to wish you a beautiful Christmas
filled with wonder and love, and I want
you to know that if I could wrap up all
these things, they would be yours today.

— Vincent Arcoleo

# This Is the Season
# for Remembering and Celebration

The holidays seem to arrive
more quickly each year,
and I find myself scrambling
for every extra minute.
But when I stop to look around,
take a deep breath
and a moment to recapture
the spirit of the season,
I remember that this is meant
to be a time of celebration.
Love and laughter are supposed
to fill these days.
That's when I remember the people
who mean so much to me —
people like you.

The holidays are for people like you:
wonderful souls who give of themselves
and put their energy into bringing
    happiness to others all year,
never asking for anything
    but love in return.

Holidays are for counting blessings,
    and I certainly count you among
the most precious of mine.
In this season, I not only send you
    warm wishes
for a beautiful celebration
and a wonderful time with family —
I also send my gratitude to you
for being better than any gift
and more valuable than
    any treasure.

— Jennifer Ellis Freeman

# You Know It's Christmas When...

You start noticing how beautiful everything is,
and you feel a little closer to nature and
   the changing of the seasons;
you get a longing in your heart
to be with people you haven't seen in a long time;
you feel closer to everyone in general;
you start thinking of things you want to do for others;
it becomes clear that your dreams
are possible, and that you will make them happen;
you feel a deeper appreciation
for all the blessings in your life,
and a desire to tell the people you love — right now —
   that you love them.

These are the things that make Christmas more
   wonderful than any other time
      of the year.

— Jessie Rose Thompson

# Christmas Returns

Christmas returns, as it always does,
with its assurance that life is good.
It is the time of lift to the spirit,
    When the mind feels its way into the commonplace,
    And senses the wonder of simple things:
    An evergreen tree,
    Familiar carols, merry laughter.
It is the time of illumination,
    When candles burn, and old dreams
    Find their youth again.
It is the time of pause,
    When forgotten joys come back to mind, and past
    Dedications renew their claim.
It is the time of harvest for the heart,
    When faith reaches out to mantle all high endeavor,
    And love whispers its magic word to everything
    That breathes.
Christmas returns, as it always does,
with its assurance that life is good.

— Howard Thurman

# May You Find These Gifts Under Your Christmas Tree

*M*ay you find HOPE.
For when all else fails, hope will lead you
on to conquer your fears and help you move
forward when you can't find a reason to.

May you find FAITH.
For faith will keep you safe, protect your
heart from pain, comfort you and relieve
your worries, see you through when you're
uncertain, and stay beside you to help when
changes come and you must adjust.

May you find PEACE.
For peace will soothe your soul, teach
you how to grow, calm you when you're
troubled, allow you to know your own
heart, and keep you following your
dreams when everything seems to fail.

May you find JOY.
For joy will give you release, encourage
you to be your best, teach you to laugh
and be free, ease your moments of pain,
and make you feel good again.

Most of all...
May you find LOVE.
For love will bring you all of the above
and even more. It will always be the only
true freedom and the only true answer.
And love will give your life all that you
could ever imagine.

— Regina Hill

# Love Is All Around Us in This Beautiful Season

You can hear the love in each Christmas melody,
for what else but love could lighten the steps
and lift the hearts of all who listen!

You can touch the love with every wrapped present,
for what else but love could select just the right gift
and conceal the surprise with beautiful paper
and lengths of ribbon!

You can see the love around every decorated tree,
for what else but love could gingerly lay the tinsel on
and gently place the angel atop!

— Phyllis Charles

# Let the Light of Christmas Fill Your Heart

When Christmas comes along,
there's something different in the air.
The world seems brighter and more beautiful.
Miracles seem possible,
love fills our hearts,
and we open our eyes to
    all the goodness surrounding us.
This holiday, let the light of Christmas fill your life.
Open your heart and receive its timeless gifts
    of peace, goodwill, hope, and love.
Surround yourself with friends, family,
    and loved ones.
Remember what matters most.
This year, celebrate the true meaning of the holiday...
and have the merriest Christmas of all.

— Rachyl Taylor

# MAY THERE BE PEACE ON EARTH

—★—

May Peace be your gift
at Christmas
and your blessing
all year through!
May peace be more than a season,
may it be a way of life!
Let the special memories
of Christmases past
bring new joy and delight
to your heart this Christmas.

— Anonymous


Before another Christmas dawns,
God grant we earn the peace
those ageless stars foretell.

— Anonymous

*P*eace is the gift we can share every day;
we can express it with the smile
we give to strangers,
in the love we share with our families,
in the optimism and concern
we give to everyone around us.
Live with peace in your own heart,
and it will shine out from there
to light the entire world.

— Edmund O'Neill

*P*eace was the first thing the angels sang.
Peace is the mark of the sons of God. Peace
is the nurse of love. Peace is the mother of
unity. Peace is the rest of blessed souls.
Peace is the dwelling place of eternity.

— Leo the Great

# THE CHRISTMAS STORY

— ★ —

Love came down at Christmas;
love all lovely, love divine;
love was born at Christmas,
stars and angels gave the sign.

— Christina G. Rossetti

Good news from heaven the angels bring,
Glad tidings to the earth they sing:
To us this day a child is given,
To crown us with the joy of heaven.

— Martin Luther

It is good to be children sometimes, and
never better than at Christmas, when its
mighty Founder was a child Himself.

— Charles Dickens

# Long, Long Ago

Winds through the olive trees
Softly did blow,
Round little Bethlehem
Long, long ago.
Sheep on the hillside lay
Whiter than snow;
Shepherds were watching them,
Long, long ago.
Then from the happy sky,
Angels bent low,
Singing their songs of joy,
Long, long ago.
For in a manger bed,
Cradled we know,
Christ came to Bethlehem,
Long, long ago.

— Anonymous

# The Art of Keeping Christmas

How can we best keep Christmas! How can we best defeat the little bit of Scrooge in all of us and experience the glory of the Great Day!

By sinking the shafts of our spirits deep beneath the sparkling tinsel of the surface of Christmas and renewing within us the radiance of the inner meaning of the season.

By following the Star on an inward journey to Bethlehem to stand again in awe and wonder before the Babe in a Manger.

By rediscovering the faith and simplicity of a little child, for of such is the Kingdom of Heaven.

By being still and listening to the angels sing within our hearts.

By quietly evaluating our lives according to the Master's standards as set forth in the Sermon on the Mount.

By reaffirming the supremacy of the spirit in man's conquest of himself.

By rededicating ourselves to the Master's ideals of Peace, Brotherhood and Good Will.

By resolving to *give ourselves away* to others in love, joy and devotion.

By using the light of Christmas to guide us through the darkness of the coming year, refusing to go back to the dim kerosene lamps of the spirit when the brilliant electricity of Christmas is available to show us the way.

— Wilferd A. Peterson

# CHRISTMAS IS...

— ★ —

Christmas is not a day or a season,
but a condition of heart and mind.
If we love our neighbors as ourselves;
if in our riches we are poor in spirit
and in our poverty we are rich in grace;
if our charity vaunteth not itself,
but suffereth long and is kind;
if when our brother asks for a loaf,
we give ourselves instead;
if each day dawns in opportunity and
sets in achievement, however small —
then every day is Christ's day and
Christmas is always near.

— James Wallingford

*W*hatever else be lost among the years,
Let us keep Christmas still a shining thing;
Whatever doubts assail us, or what fears,
Let us hold close one day, remembering
Its poignant meaning for the hearts of men.
Let us get back our childlike faith again.

— Grace Noll Crowell

*S*o remember while December
Brings the Christmas day,
In the year let there be Christmas
In the things you do and say;
Wouldn't life be worth the living
Wouldn't dreams be coming true
If we kept the Christmas spirit
All the whole year through!

— Anonymous

# HOME FOR THE HOLIDAYS

---  ★  ---

*I* do come home at Christmas. We all do, or we all
should. We all come home, or ought to come home,
for a short holiday — the longer, the better — from the
great boarding school where we are forever working at
our arithmetical slates, to take, and give a rest.

— Charles Dickens

*T*he best Christmas of all is the presence of a
happy family all wrapped up with one another.

— Anonymous

*F*rom home to home, and heart to heart,
from one place to another...
The warmth and joy of Christmas
brings us closer to each other...

— Emily Matthews

The best feeling in this world is family.
From it, we draw love,
    friendship, moral support,
and the fulfillment of every
    special need within our hearts.
In a family, we are connected to
    an ever-present source
of sunny moments, smiles and laughter,
understanding and encouragement,
and hugs that help us grow
    in confidence all along life's path.
Wherever we are,
whatever we're doing,
whenever we really need to feel
    especially loved, befriended,
        supported, and cared for
            in the greatest way,
our hearts can turn to the family
and find the very best
    always waiting for us.

— Barbara J. Hall

# Do You Remember Christmas when You were Little?

Wasn't Christmas wonderful when you were little? You just knew Santa would not fail to put something delightful under the tree. Because you were a child, the music and the stories and the wonder of Christmas were yours — you belonged to the land where it all came from. You just jumped in and lived it.

Do you remember the feeling of trying to be so quiet while you looked for hidden presents before Christmas? And the excitement and curiosity about what was in those packages? And when Christmas Day finally came and you got to open them, how surprised you were, because you thought you had guessed what was in every package.

Remember how very excited you were when you made something all by yourself for someone special, and you just couldn't wait for them to open it and see what you had made them! Your first experience was the warm and happy feeling of knowing you had made someone else happy. That was the very best part.

But the most wonderful thing about Christmas was hearing laughter and listening to the bustle and the talk, and feeling all the warmth of home, with the smiles on the faces of your family somehow making everything just right. Because Christmas is a time for sharing love. And when you felt that indescribable feeling, the one that made you glow from the inside out, you knew without any doubt at all that you belonged, and that you were a part of something very, very special. That is what Christmas is all about.

— Judith L. Sloan

# The Best Kind of Presents

The priceless gifts of Christmas
are not the ones wrapped
or placed under the tree,
but the gifts we give when
we give of ourselves.
It is the love that we share.
It is the comfort we lend at times of need.
It is the moments we spend together
helping each other follow our dreams.
The most priceless gifts of Christmas
are the understanding and caring
that come from the heart.
And each and every one of us
has these gifts to offer...
through the gift of ourselves.

— Ben Daniels

*S*omehow not only for Christmas
But all the long year through,
The joy that you give to others
Is the joy that comes back to you.
And the more you spend in blessing
The poor, and lonely and sad,
The more of your heart's possessing
Returns to make you glad.

— John Greenleaf Whittier


*M*ay you have the gladness of Christmas
    which is hope;
The spirit of Christmas
    which is peace;
The heart of Christmas
    which is love.

— Ada V. Hendricks

# My Special Wishes
# for a Special Person This Christmas

Naturally, I hope Santa's good to you this Christmas, but I have some other wishes for you, too, that can't be wrapped up in a pretty package and tied with a matching bow… I wish you love in your life, hope in your heart, faith in your dreams, and encouragement enough to do whatever would make you happy, keep you healthy, and assure you the prosperity you deserve.

I wish you joy. I wish you peace. I wish you blessings in your life. I wish you answers to questions, resolve to change something that you want to change, and the awareness and ability to accept something that perhaps you haven't been able to change.

I wish you satisfaction in your work and all the other things that would make your day-to-day life more balanced and content and rewarding. I wish you happiness in your family, unconditional love for each other, and understanding. I wish you the capacity and knowledge to embrace the gift of love that dwells in your heart and that is replenished when given away.

Everyone is unique and different. I hope you can appreciate your own uniqueness and realize that you're an angel in disguise to some, a friend so important to others, and a member of a family with whom you have significance and importance beyond description.

Special people help us to change our lives, make us feel good about ourselves, and therefore enhance our potential to realize our dreams. They give us a sense of community and belonging. They make us feel appreciated and accepted and move us toward our own emotional security.

If whatever you're wishing for this Christmas is not covered in these special wishes from my heart to yours, I wish for you your heart's desire because you're so special to me. May God bless you and keep you during this special season.

— Donna Fargo

# Day of Hope

Christmas is the one day of the year that carries real
hope and promise for all mankind.
It carries the torch of brotherhood.
It is the one day in the year when most of us grow big
of heart and broad of mind.
It is the single day when most of us are as kind and as
thoughtful of others as we know how to be;
when most of us are as gracious and generous as we
would like always to be;
when the joy of the home is more important than the
profits of the office;
when peoples of all races speak cheerfully to each other
when they meet;
when high and low wish each other well;
and the one day when even enemies forgive
and forget.

— Edgar A. Guest

# Christmas Is a Miracle

In an age dominated by science, with emphasis upon the actual and literal, we tend to scoff at dreams and miracles. Christmas encourages and reinforces these parts of our nature. It brings out the spirituality we sense within, conjures up images we know from memories too deeply a part of our universal consciousness to ever fade.

— Leo Buscaglia

Though there are many miracles during the Christmas holidays, the blessing of children is the greatest one of all. It is in their eyes that we see the spirit of Christmas reflected.

— Josie Willis

# *Christmas Brings Us All Together*

Christmas is the bringing together of our most heartfelt and happy thoughts. It is thinking of those we care so much about. It is the cherishing of memories through the years, and it is looking forward to the blessings that lie ahead.

Christmas is the quiet appreciation of times together, of making everything better, and of feelings that glow like candles in the window. Christmas is a time of the year that has been so golden in its yesterdays and is so hopeful as it travels on its way toward tomorrow.

Christmas is a prayer that keeps us close and blesses us with a gentle recognition of all that we are.

Christmas is you and me in this world,
    wishing on the very same star.

— Douglas Pagels

When Christmas bells are swinging
above the fields of snow,
We hear sweet voices ringing
from lands of long ago,
And etched on vacant places
Are half-forgotten faces
Of friends we used to cherish,
and loves we used to know —
when Christmas bells are swinging
above the fields of snow.

— Ella Wheeler Wilcox


The charm of Christmas lies in
the thought that we live in the
memory of our friends.

— Anonymous

# The Magic of This Season...

If the music stopped
and the presents disappeared
if the dog ate the cookies
if there was no glitter one year
if the bells went on strike
and the reindeer quit
if Santa Claus changed his name
when his clothes wouldn't fit
if the snow wouldn't snow
and the malls closed their doors
if the gingerbread houses collapsed
to the floor

If we didn't have holiday sales anymore
and there weren't any wreaths
or plum puddings or s'mores
if the trees stayed outside
and the elves went away
if there were no molasses
to compare to the wait

If all of the trappings and wrappings
and bows
got locked in a warehouse
beyond the North Pole
and the best we could hope for
was one single note
from the piano (for carols)
that suddenly broke...

and if Christmas arrived, unannounced
in this way
with no drummers, no banner
no Christmas parade
it would not make a difference
No — it would not change the way
that the heart skips a beat
at the sound of a sleigh
or a car pulling into a familiar
driveway
knowing Christmas — yes
And coming home.

— Ashley Rice

# Remember the Spirit of Christmas

Are you willing to stoop down and consider
  the needs and the desires of little children;
to remember the weakness and loneliness of
  people who are growing old;
to stop asking how much your friends love
  you, and ask yourself whether you love
  them enough;
to bear in mind the things that other people
  have to bear in their hearts;
to try to understand what those who live in
  the same home with you really want,
  without waiting for them to tell you;
to trim your lamp so that it will give more
  light and less smoke, and to carry it in
front so that your shadow will fall behind
  you;

Are you willing to make a grave for your ugly
    thoughts, and a garden for your good thoughts,
    with the gate open —
are you willing to do these things even for a day?
Then you can keep Christmas.
Are you willing to believe that love is the strongest
    thing in the world — stronger than hate, stronger
    than evil, stronger than death — and that the
    blessed life which began in Bethlehem nineteen
    hundred years ago is the image and brightness of
    the Eternal Love?
Then you can keep Christmas.
And if you keep it for a day, why not always?

— Henry van Dyke

# Christmas Is a Time for New Beginnings

Christmas is a time for reflection as well as celebration.
As you look back on the past year and all that has
    taken place in your life,
remember each experience for the good that has come of it
    and for the knowledge you have gained.
Remember the efforts you have made and the goals
    you have reached.
Remember the love you have shared and the happiness
    you have brought.
Remember the laughter, the joy, the hard work,
    and the tears.

And as you reflect on the past year, also be thinking of
    the new one to come.
Because most importantly, Christmas is a time of birth,
    new beginnings, and the celebration of life.

— Taylor Addison

# The Way to a Happy New Year

To leave the old with a burst of song;
To recall the right and forgive the wrong;
To forget the things that bind you fast
To the vain regrets of the year that's past;
To have the strength to let go your hold
Of the not worth while of the days grown old;
To dare go forth with a purpose true,
To the unknown task of the year that's new;
To help your brother along the road,
To do his work and lift his load;
To add your gift to the world's good cheer,
Is to have and to give a Happy New Year.

— Anonymous

# May You Always Have
# a Christmas Angel by Your Side

May you always have an angel by your side 🌿
Watching out for you in all the things you do 🌿
Reminding you to keep believing in brighter days 🌿
Finding ways for your wishes and dreams to take
you to beautiful places 🌿 Giving you hope that is
as certain as the sun 🌿 Giving you the strength of
serenity as your guide 🌿 May you always have love
and comfort and courage 🌿

And may you always have an angel by your side 🌿
Someone there to catch you if you fall 🌿 Encouraging
your dreams 🌿 Inspiring your happiness 🌿 Holding
your hand and helping you through it all 🌿

In all of our days, our lives are always changing ✺
Tears come along as well as smiles ✺ Along the roads
you travel, may the miles be a thousand times more
lovely than lonely ✺ May they give you gifts that
never, ever end: someone wonderful to love and a
dear friend in whom you can confide ✺ May you
have rainbows after every storm ✺ May you have
hopes to keep you warm ✺

✺And may you always have an angel by your side ✺

— Douglas Pagels

# You're Thought of at Christmas and Every Day of the Year

Today, I wish you love —
the kind that celebrates
all the special moments
the holidays can bring.
I wish you hope —
the kind that sees
a year full of dreams come true.
I wish you peace —
the kind that is
as warm and special as you are.
I wish you joy —
the kind that is wrapped
in all the happiness you deserve.
I wish you everything
the Christmas season brings.

— Linda E. Knight

# To Someone Very Special at Christmas

As Christmas feelings warm the heart and the year gently comes to a close, I want to share this joyful feeling... as a way of saying a lasting "thank you" and passing along a loving reminder that I appreciate you so much...

for the many, many blessings
   with which you have touched
      my life.

You are so wonderful, and...
the closeness I have with you
   will always be...

one of the most important
   things in the whole
      world to me.

— Marin McKay

# Acknowledgments

We gratefully acknowledge the permission granted by the following authors, publishers, and authors' representatives to reprint poems or excerpts from their publications.

The Estate of Howard Thurman for "Christmas Returns" from THE MOOD OF CHRISTMAS by Howard Thurman, published by Harper & Row Publishers. Copyright © 1974 by Howard Thurman. All rights reserved.

Regina Hill for "May You Find These Gifts Under Your Christmas Tree." Copyright © 2002 by Regina Hill. All rights reserved.

The Heacock Literary Agency for "The Art of Keeping Christmas" from THE ART OF LIVING TREASURE CHEST by Wilferd A. Peterson, published by Simon & Schuster, Inc. Copyright © 1977 by Wilferd A. Peterson. All rights reserved.

"Whatever else be lost among the years..." from SONGS OF HOPE by Grace Noll Crowell. Copyright © 1938 by Harper & Brothers. Renewed 1966 by Grace Noll Crowell. All rights reserved.

Judith L. Sloan for "Do You Remember Christmas When You Were Little!" Copyright © 2002 by Judith L. Sloan. All rights reserved.

PrimaDonna Entertainment Corp. for "My Special Wishes for a Special Person This Christmas" by Donna Fargo. Copyright © 1999 by PrimaDonna Entertainment Corp. All rights reserved.

The Bowery Mission for "Day of Hope" by Edgar A. Guest, published in *Christian Herald* (December 1946). Copyright © 1946 by Edgar A. Guest. All rights reserved.

Slack Incorporated for "In an age dominated by science..." from SEVEN STORIES OF CHRISTMAS LOVE by Leo Buscaglia. Copyright © 1987 by Leo Buscaglia, Inc. All rights reserved.

A careful effort has been made to trace the ownership of selections used in this anthology in order to obtain permission to reprint copyrighted material and give proper credit to the copyright owners. If any error or omission has occurred, it is completely inadvertent, and we would like to make corrections in future editions provided that written notification is made to the publisher:

BLUE MOUNTAIN ARTS, INC., P.O. Box 4549, Boulder, Colorado 80306.